The Illustrated Story of President

WILFORD WOODRUFF

Great Leaders of The Church
of Jesus Christ of Latter-day Saints

The Illustrated Story of President Wilford Woodruff
Great Leaders of The Church of Jesus Christ
of Latter-day Saints

Copyright © 1982 by
Eagle Systems International
P.O. Box 508
Provo, Utah 84603

ISBN: 0-938762-04-4
Library of Congress Catalog Card No.: 82-70689

Fourth Printing April 1987

First Edition

All rights reserved. No part of this publication may be reproduced or used in any manner or by any means—graphic, electronic, or mechanical, including photocopying, recording, taping, or information storage and retrieval systems—without written permission of the publisher.

Lithographed in U.S.A.
by
COMMUNITY PRESS, INC.

A Member of
The American Bookseller's Association
New York, New York

The Illustrated Story of President

WILFORD WOODRUFF

Great Leaders of The Church
of Jesus Christ of Latter-day Saints

AUTHOR
Annette C. Hullinger

ILLUSTRATOR
B. Keith Christensen

DIRECTOR AND CORRELATOR
Lael J. Woodbury

ADVISORS AND EDITORS
Paul & Millie Cheesman
Mark Ray Davis
L. Norman Egan
Annette Hullinger
Beatrice W. Friel

PUBLISHER
Steven R. Shallenberger

A Biography Of WILFORD WOODRUFF

President Wilford Woodruff, fourth President of The Church of Jesus Christ of Latter-day Saints, was born in Farmington, Connecticut, on March 1, 1807.

He lived in an area where the people were very strict about religion. Wilford began his study of the Bible at an early age, and he developed great faith in God. His love for his Father in Heaven and the Savior prompted him to search and pray constantly for the true Church.

He read some negative reports about Mormonism in the newspapers, but later he met Latter-day Saint missionaries in Richland, New York, where he and his brother Azmon had gone to work. Through the spirit of the Holy Ghost he recognized the truth for which he had been searching. He was baptized in water mixed with snow and ice on December 31, 1833.

Soon after his baptism he was called to serve on the first of several missions. Because of his powerful faith, determination, and his ability to follow the Spirit, he became an outstanding missionary in the Church.

During the lifetime of the Prophet Joseph Smith, President Woodruff became known as "Wilford the Faithful." This title appropriately describes the life he lived. He kept the commandments to the best of his ability and did what was asked of him with a willing heart. He served the Lord with total commitment.

He suffered many accidents and illnesses during his life, but through the protective care of a loving Heavenly Father, he was miraculously preserved to fulfill his great calling.

He was ordained an apostle by Brigham Young at Far West, Missouri, on April 26, 1839, at the age of thirty-two. He served as an apostle until April 7, 1889, when he was sustained President of the Church. He was then eighty-two years old.

Although the Church was under much stress and persecution during the time he was president, President Woodruff persistently moved its work forward. His gospel messages strengthened and blessed the lives of the Saints during their hardships.

President Woodruff lived the law of plural marriage. He had five wives and was the father of thirty-three children. He loved being home with his family and found great peace and joy during the time he spent with them.

On September 2, 1898, President Woodruff died while convalescing in San Francisco, California, at the age of ninety-one.

Winter kept the little town of Farmington, Connecticut, snuggly tucked in with a deep, white blanket of fluffy snow. The air was crisp and chill and the only sign of warmth came from the chimney smoke lazily curling its way through the biting cold air. Spring was in no hurry as far as the outside world was concerned, but to the family of Aphek and Beulah Thompson Woodruff, March 1, 1807, brought a special touch of spring warmth. Inside their cozy home a tiny new son was born. Four-year-old Azmon and two-year-old Thompson stared in wonderment at their new little playmate. He was not exactly what Thompson had expected him to be.

"Can he talk?" whispered Thompson, touching his tiny fingers gently.

"Newborn babies can't talk, Thompson," responded Azmon, using his older, wiser tone of voice. "Babies have to grow up big like us before they can walk and talk and play with their big brothers. All he can do now is eat, sleep, and cry."

Time passed slowly at first for the two brothers, but it wasn't long before they noticed the first tooth. Then came the day that Wilford could crawl and say a few words. How exciting it was for the whole family to have a baby to enjoy. Azmon and Thompson found a new kind of excitement, though, when baby Wilford began to walk and found their toys more fascinating than his own! Sometimes they even found themselves wanting to bring back the quieter days when all their baby brother could do was eat, sleep, and cry.

The peace and happiness of the young Woodruff family was suddenly interrupted when Wilford was just fifteen months old. His mother, who was a young woman twenty-eight years old, became ill with spotted fever and died. The joy and happiness that once filled their home seemed to be gone forever. Life was so lonely without her. There was no mother to kiss a skinned knee or rock them to sleep. There was no mother's goodnight kiss to sweeten the night's dreams. What were they to do without a mother to take care of them?

They were not left in sorrow too long. Their father met and married Azbah Hart. Their new mother was a good, kind woman with a warm smile and twinkling eyes that showed the love she felt for them. When she held them snuggly in her arms, their fears and worries melted away. Her love and devotion blessed the lives of her three new sons and brought back the softness of a mother's touch that the little boys had so deeply missed.

Six more children were born into the Woodruff family, and they grew in love and happiness, as well as size.

While life was filled with many happy times, Wilford soon learned that it had its dangerous, painful experiences, too. When he was three years old, he fell into a large kettle of scalding water. Although he was instantly rescued, he was so badly burned that it took nine long months before his life was out of danger. This was only the beginning of many accidents and illnesses that would threaten the life of this great prophet.

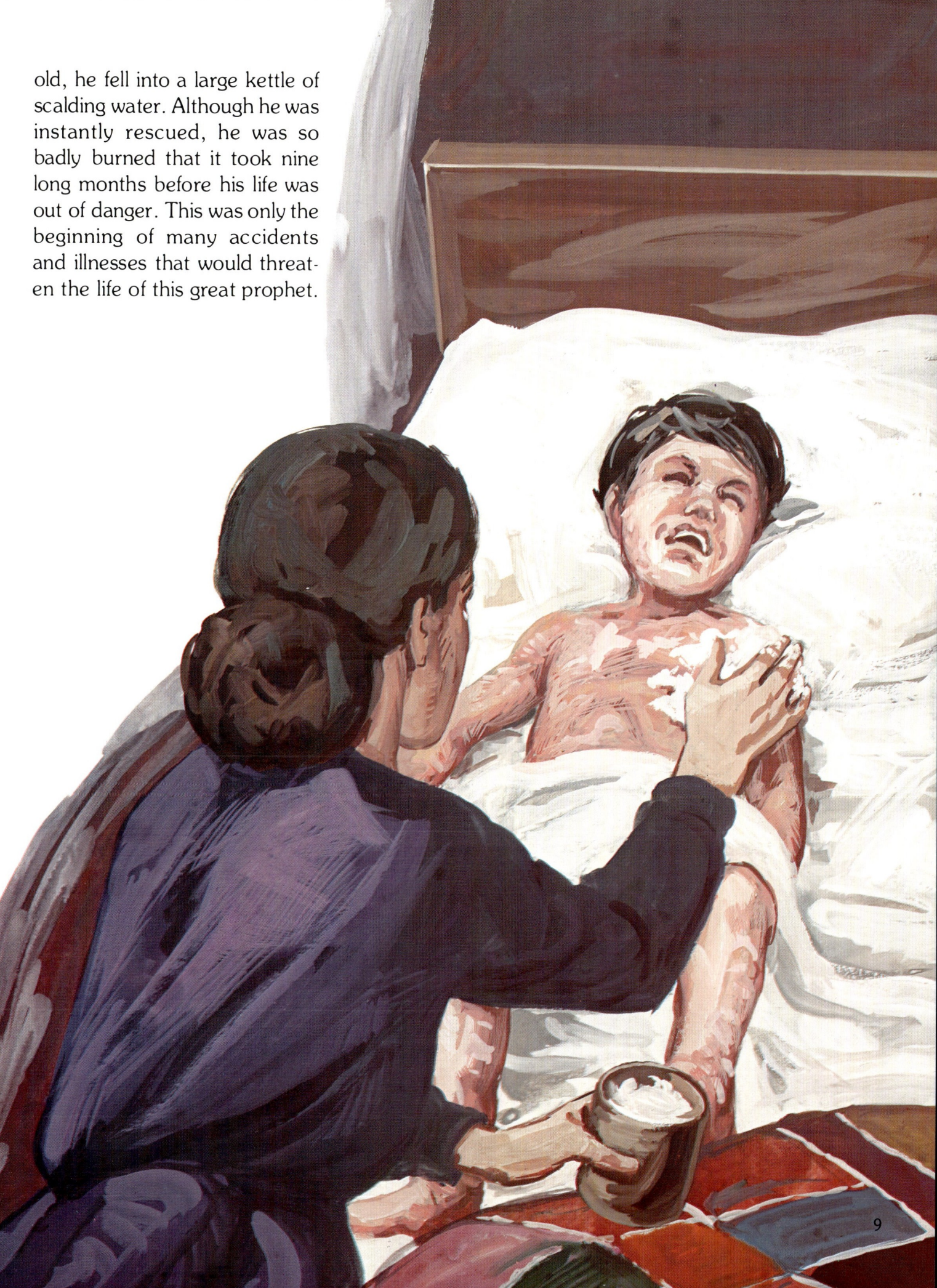

Several accidents occurred during his fifth and sixth years. One day he and his older brothers went into the barn to play.

"Beat you to the top of the hayloft," challenged Azmon. The race was on! No sooner had they reached the top than a loud scream shattered the air. Wilford had fallen from a beam and landed on his face on the bare floor several feet below. He was badly hurt, but he recovered shortly and was once again joining his brothers in new adventures.

Just as you and I must sometimes learn obedience to parents the hard way, young Wilford had this lesson to learn, too. One Saturday evening Wilford and his two brothers, Azmon and Thompson, were looking for something exciting to do. "Hey," Thompson whispered, "why don't we sneak up into the attic and play?"

"We can't do that, Thompson," cautioned Azmon. "You know that father warned us never to play up there. It's dangerous!"

"Oh, come on, Azmon," begged Wilford. "We won't stay long."

Up the steep stairs they ran. Wilford was nearly to the top when he missed a step and fell clear to the bottom of the stairs. "My arm, my arm!" he cried. He had never felt such pain! "I'm dying . . . oh, my arm!" Sure enough, the arm was broken. Wilford thought the pain would last his whole life. When it was finally healed, he promised himself that he would never again suffer because of disobedience to his parents.

Promises can sometimes be forgotten, and like many children, he had another lesson to learn about the value of obeying parents. One evening shortly after his arm had healed, Wilford was feeding pumpkins to his father's heard of horned cattle. Included in the herd was a very ill-tempered bull, who had no friends, man or beast. Besides being unfriendly, the bull was also selfish, a trait that Wilford disliked, even as a boy.

As any selfish bull would do, he promptly left his pumpkin and took the one that Wilford had just fed to his favorite cow. Wilford was not about to tolerate that selfish act. He quickly picked up the bull's pumpkin to give it to the cow. That would show him! No sooner did he get the pumpkin in his arms, however, than the angry bull came plunging after him. Down the hill ran Wilford, with the bull right at his heels. Just then his father looked up and, seeing the danger, yelled, "Wilford, throw down the pumpkin! Throw down the pumpkin!" Wilford's dislike for the bull and determination caused him to momentarily forget his resolution to be obedient, and he held on tighter. Then, with a big thud, he fell flat on the ground and the pumpkin rolled out of his arms. The bull leaped over the frightened boy and tore the pumpkin to pieces. Once again Wilford had been protected by his Father in Heaven.

Before he was twenty years old, he had broken both arms and a leg, fallen from a tree flat onto his back, and been kicked in the stomach by an ox. He had been nearly smothered when a load of hay fell on him and had had a frightening ride on a runaway horse, had nearly drowned, and had come very close to being frozen to death. He had slit his foot open with an ax and had been bitten on the hand by a rabid dog. His life had been continually plagued with accidents and illnesses.

Of these life-threatening experiences he once said, "Evidently, I have been numbered with those who are apparently the marked victims of misfortunes. It has seemed to me at times as though some invisible power were watching my footsteps in search of an opportunity to destroy my life. I, therefore, ascribe my preservation on earth to the watchcare of a merciful Providence, whose hand has been stretched out to rescue me from death when I was in the presence of the most threatening dangers."

Wilford became aware that Satan would like to destroy him and keep him from the great work he was foreordained to do, but he knew that he was a child of God and that his Father in Heaven would always protect and care for him. His great desire in life was to serve Heavenly Father and to be worthy of the protective care and guidance he received.

Young Wilford's love for Heavenly Father and his thirst for truth grew stronger through his personal study of the Bible. He had great faith, even at an early age, and had a great desire to keep the commandments and do the things he felt the Lord would want him to do.

Wilford's religious beliefs differed from those of the people where he lived. They did not believe in having prophets, apostles, or revelation. Wilford thought, "Surely the principles of the gospel of Jesus Christ that were important in the time of Christ are just as important in any period of time. They are important now and forever."

Wilford had an old friend named Robert Mason who believed as he did. The old man would come to the Woodruff home and talk about religion with Wilford and his brothers. The last day that Wilford spent with his old friend, he told Wilford about a dream he felt compelled by the Spirit to share with him. It had been made known to him that the Lord's Church was not organized on the earth among the men of his generation, but it would be on the earth during his children's generation. He then said, "Wilford, I shall never enjoy the blessings of the church in this life, but you will become an important person in the new kingdom."

This made a great impression on young Wilford, and he prayed continually for the Lord to lead him by the Spirit and prepare him for his Church, when it did come.

After working with his father in the flour and sawmills for several years, Wilford and his brother Azmon left Connecticut and went to New York to work.

On December 29, 1833, Wilford returned home from work to find his sister-in-law waiting anxiously to share some good news. "Elders Zera Pulsipher and Elijah Cheney, missionaries from the Mormon Church, came to our door today," she began. "It seems they're preaching at the schoolhouse in the village tonight. I told them that I thought you and Azmon would be there to listen to them since you two are always talking about religion."

An excited Wilford quickly turned out his horses and headed for the schoolhouse without even waiting for supper. His soul craved the spiritual nourishment he was anticipating from this meeting! On the way he prayed, "Father, please help me to know if these men are of thee and whether or not the doctrines they teach are true. If they are, I pray that thou wilt prepare my heart to receive their message."

When he arrived, the schoolhouse was already packed, and he found his brother Azmon was already there. The missionaries prayed, taught the gospel, and bore witness of the truth of the Book of Mormon. As they taught, the Spirit bore witness to Wilford that he had indeed found the truth. The witness of the Holy Ghost gave him a warm, peaceful feeling inside. His soul had found the peace and harmony he had so earnestly prayed for.

On December 31, 1833, Wilford and Azmon were baptized by Elder Pulsipher. Of his baptism Wilford writes, "The snow was about three feet deep, the day was cold, and the water was mixed with ice and snow, yet I did not feel the cold." From that day forward his pursuit of righteousness was never hindered by cold, illness, or severe persecution. The gift of the Holy Ghost he received that day became the most powerful influence in his life.

THINK ABOUT IT:

1. What are some of the lessons Wilford had to learn about being obedient to his parents?
2. How had Wilford prepared himself in his early life to recognize the truth when the missionaries taught him?
3. What are some of the experiences in Wilford's life that showed him that Heavenly Father loved him and was protecting him?

Four months after his baptism Wilford went to Kirtland, Ohio, and met the Prophet Joseph Smith. He found the Prophet to be a man whose love could be felt in a handshake. From that first meeting until the time of the Prophet's death their friendship was one of mutual love and trust.

Now that Wilford had found the gospel, he was anxious to share his happiness with other people. He wanted to go on a mission and take the gospel to others, but he felt it was not right to ask for that privilege. He knew that he needed to be called by the Lord to do missionary work. His desire and faith led him into a nearby woods to pray for the opportunity to preach the gospel to the world.

"Before I rose from my knees," he said, "the spirit of the Lord rested upon me and bore witness that my prayer was heard and should be answered upon my head. I arose very happy and walked through thick woods about 600 feet onto an open road. As I entered the roadway, I met Judge Elias Higbee. Brother Higbee was a high priest and a very faithful man, one of the noblest men of God in the last days. . . . To my surprise, as soon as I approached him he said, 'Brother Woodruff, the spirit of the Lord tells me that you should be ordained to go and preach the gospel.'" Wilford's prayer had been answered and he felt like he would burst with joy!

He was ordained a priest on November 5, 1834, and received his call to serve in the Southern states. His life of missionary service began just eight days later. He left with a few Books of Mormon, very little clothing, and enough teaching desire to fill the whole world! He would trust in the Lord for his food and a place to sleep each night.

Wilford and his companion had to travel through the state of Missouri, where the Mormons were deeply hated. They decided it may not be wise to stop there and ask for food or a place to sleep. Instead of taking a chance on being killed, they slept on the cold, hard ground without blanket or sheet. They picked some corn in a field as they walked through and ate it raw. This was only the beginning of many exciting and sometimes discouraging missionary experiences of Wilford Woodruff. It didn't seem to matter to him what he had to suffer, Wilford's love for his Father in Heaven and the gospel overcame all of the problems he had to face. The great joy he felt each time someone accepted the truth of the gospel kept him encouraged in his missionary work.

One morning Wilford and his companion started their day's journey without any food at all, not knowing what was ahead. Wilford describes this experience, "We started about sunrise and crossed a thirty-mile prairie, apparently as level as a house floor, without shrub or water. We arrived at timber about two o'clock in the afternoon.

"As we approached the timber, a large black bear came out towards us. We were not afraid of him, for we were on the Lord's business, and had not mocked God's prophets as did the forty-two wicked children who said to Elisha, 'Go up thou bald head.' for which they were torn by bears. When the bear got within 132 ft. of us he sat on his haunches, looked at us a moment, and ran away; and we went on our way rejoicing.

"We had to travel in the night, which was cloudy and very dark, so we had great difficulty to keep the road. Soon a large drove of wolves gathered around, and followed us. They came very close, and at times it seemed as though they would eat us up. We had materials for striking a light, and at ten o'clock, not knowing where we were, and the wolves becoming so bold, we thought it wisdom to make a fire; so we stopped and gathered a lot of oak limbs that lay on the ground, and lit them, and as our fire began to burn, the wolves left us."

After four months of these difficult and trying experiences, Wilford's companion left him sitting on a log in an alligator swamp with a sharp pain in his knee that caused him to be lame. Wilford could have given up, too, and many people would not have heard the gospel. Instead of giving up and going home, he quietly knelt down in the mud and prayed. Telling of his experience, he said simply, "The Lord healed me and I went on my way rejoicing." It was this kind of faith, determination, and positive attitude that made him an outstanding missionary in the history of the Church. Although his missionary path was always full of problems, he would never give up.

When Wilford reached his thirtieth birthday, he met Phoebe Whittemore Carter from the state of Maine. She and other members of her family had been baptized earlier. They soon fell in love and were married. She was a gracious, loving wife and continually encouraged and supported him in all that he did. She also went with him to teach the gospel whenever she could.

Wilford had been called first to the Second Quorum of Seventy. At the age of twenty-nine he was called to the First Quorum of Seventy, and at the age of thirty-two he was called to be an apostle of the Lord. He felt very humbled to think that the Lord had that much faith and trust in him.

On the same day that he was called to be an apostle, he and the rest of the Quorum of the Twelve were called to serve a mission to England. This was his third mission. His first had been to the Southern states, and the second had included the Fox Islands, just off the coast of Maine, and the Eastern states.

The Twelve Apostles spent several months getting ready for this mission. During this time they received spiritual strength and learned the doctrines of the Church from the Prophet Joseph Smith. He loved these good men and promised them that if they were faithful, they would be blessed during their missions, bring many people into the Church, and return home safely.

As the departure day for the Twelve came closer, nearly all of the apostles or their families became very sick with chills and fever or other illnesses.

Wilford and Phoebe became very ill with chills and fever. Finally, after suffering in bed for thirteen days, Wilford got up, packed his things, and prepared to leave. He was still very weak and ill, but he was determined to leave on schedule.

"Early upon the morning of the 8th of August," he wrote, "I arose from my bed of sickness, laid my hands upon the head of my sick wife, Phoebe, and blessed her. I then departed from the embrace of my companion, and left her almost without food or the necessities of life. She suffered my departure with the fortitude that becomes a saint, realizing the responsibilities of her companion. I quote from my journal; 'Phoebe, farewell! Be of good cheer; remember me in your prayers. I leave these pages for your perusal when I am gone. I shall see your face again in the flesh. I go to obey the commands of Jesus Christ.'"

His mission to England began in Preston, an area where there were many factories.

One evening after he had been there a short time, he met with a large group of the Saints and others who were there to hear him teach the gospel. While singing the opening hymn, the Spirit of the Lord told him that this would be the last meeting he would hold with these people for many days. He was very surprised because he had made many appointments to teach the gospel in that area. He baptized four people at the close of the meeting.

In the morning Wilford knelt in prayer to ask the Lord where he would like him to go. The answer that he received was that he should travel south, for the Lord had a great work for him to do there. The next morning he left for Herefordshire.

This was a farming area that had never been visited by the missionaries. There he met a wealthy farmer, John Benbow, who, with his wife, Jane, welcomed him with great happiness. Said John, "There is a large group of people here—over six hundred—who have broken off from the Wesleyan Methodists, and have taken the name of United Brethren. They have forty-five preachers among them, and for religious services have chapels and many houses that are licensed according to the law of the land. They are calling upon the Lord continually to open the way before them and send light and knowledge, that they might know the true way to be saved."

When Wilford heard this, he knew exactly why the Lord had sent him to Herefordshire. He was so excited and happy, he could hardly sleep. Just imagine the joy and happiness he felt. He knew that the Lord had brought him here with the truth these people had been praying for. He knelt and thanked the Lord for this special blessing.

He began preaching early the next morning and into the evening. His heart was full of gratitude as he looked into the faces of all those good people who were seeking the truths of the gospel.

Word spread, and after two days, six hundred people were baptized. Word also spread to the local preacher, who became very angry when he learned that Wilford Woodruff's congregation numbered a thousand, while only fifteen people were attending his meetings. He decided he'd better do something fast!

The next morning when Wilford stood before the people to preach, a man came in the door and informed him that he was the local constable and had been sent by the preacher to arrest him. "For what crime?" Wilford asked. "For preaching to the people," was the reply. "But sir," explained Wilford, "I have a license to preach the gospel to these people. However, if you will just sit down in this chair and wait until the meeting is over, we will talk about this misunderstanding and get it settled."

At the close of the meeting Wilford invited all of those who desired baptism to come forward. Among those who wanted to be baptized were four ministers and the constable.

Following his baptism, the constable returned to the preacher and said, "If you want Mr. Woodruff taken in for preaching the gospel, you must go and serve the writ yourself; for I have heard him preach the only true gospel sermon I have ever listened to in my life."

"Be on your way," yelled the preacher. "I'll find another way!" He thought for a minute and then said, "I have it! I'll send two clerks from the

Church of England to spy on him and find out exactly what it is that this man, Woodruff, is teaching. I'm sure I can do better than he can—after all, I'm older and far more experienced!"

When the clerks heard the gospel, the Holy Ghost bore witness to them that they had heard the truth, and they were baptized. The preacher wisely decided that he had better not send anyone else.

Despite the opposition, Wilford continued to teach the gospel and baptize new members each day. There was no opposition too strong for the witness of the Holy Ghost that the people felt as they listened to the truth. In just eight months eighteen hundred people had accepted the gospel. Two hundred ministers from other churches and all but one member of the United Brethren were included in that number.

Of this mission, Wilford says, "The power of God rested upon us and upon the mission. The sick were healed, devils were cast out, and the lame made to walk. The whole history of this Herefordshire mission shows the importance of listening to the still small voice of the spirit of God, and the revelations of the Holy Ghost. The people were praying for the light and truth, and the Lord sent me to them. In all these things we should ever acknowledge the hand of God, and give Him the honor, praise, and glory forever and ever."

Though his missionary service through the years kept him from his family and friends for months at a time, and though his trials and persecutions would have caused many men to weaken and give up, Wilford Woodruff's faith and obedience moved him constantly forward. He developed the strong characteristics that the Lord requires of his prophets through his determination and dedication in doing whatever the Lord asked him to do with a willing heart. The Lord's will became his will, no matter how hard it was for him. He knew the Lord would be with him.

One of the greatest blessings and joys of his missionary service came when he converted his parents, brothers, sister, and his relatives. He had been promised in his patriarical blessing, given in April, 1837, that he would bring all of his family into the Church. With the help of the Lord, he saw this promise fulfilled.

Wilford had learned to listen to the promptings of the Spirit, and because he did, he had many special experiences. One of these experiences happened in 1848 when he was appointed by the Presidency of the Church to take his family and go to Boston to lead some of the Saints west. "While on my way east," he said, "I put my carriage into the yard of one of the brethren in Indiana, and Brother Orson Hyde set his wagon by the side of mine, and not more than two feet from it.

"Dominicus Carter, of Provo, and my wife and four children were with me. My wife, one child and I went to bed in the carriage, the rest sleeping in the house. I had been in bed but a short time when a voice said to me: 'Get up, and move your carriage.' It was not thunder, lightening or an earthquake, but the still, small voice of the Spirit of God—the Holy Ghost.

"I told my wife I must get up and move my carriage. She asked, 'What for?' I told her I did not know, only the Spirit told me to do it. I got up and moved my carriage

several feet, and set it by the side of the house.

"As I was returning to bed the same Spirit said to me, 'Go and move your mules away from that oak tree,' which was about one hundred yards north of our carriage. I moved them to a young hickory grove and tied them up. I then went to bed.

"In thirty minutes a whirlwind caught the tree to which my mules had been fastened, broke it off near the ground, and carried it one hundred yards, sweeping away two fences in its course, and laid it prostrate through that yard where my carriage stood, and the top limbs hit my carriage as it was.

"In the morning I measured the trunk of the tree which fell where my carriage had stood, and I found it to be five feet in diameter. It came within a foot of Brother Hyde's wagon, but did not touch it. Thus, by obeying the revelation of the Spirit of God to me, I saved my life and the lives of my wife and child, as well as my animals."

"While returning to Utah in 1850 with a large company of Saints from Boston and the east, on my arrival at Pittsburg I engaged a passage for myself and company on a steamer to St. Louis. But no sooner had I engaged the passage than the Spirit said to me, 'Go not on board of that steamer, neither you nor your company.' I obeyed the revelation to me, and did not go on board, but took another steamer.

"The first steamer started at dark, with 200 passengers on board. When five miles down the Ohio River it took fire, burned the tiller ropes so that the vessel could not reach shore, and the lives of nearly all on board were lost either by fire or water. We arrived in safety at our destination, by obeying the revelation of the Spirit of God to us." This kind of obedience to the promptings of the Spirit were characteristic of the life of Wilford Woodruff.

At the time Joseph Smith organized the Council of the Twelve, he asked each of them to keep a journal of their lives. Wilford did as the Prophet asked. Not only did he keep thousands of pages telling about his own life, but he also kept a record of the sermons and teachings of Joseph Smith and the important events that took place in the early days of the Church. If he had not been obedient and kept this journal, many things of spiritual and historical value would have been lost.

Wilford loved the temples and the sacred ordinances that were performed in them. He participated in the dedications of several of the temples and was President of the St. George Temple. While he was President of the St. George Temple, he worked hard to make sure the temple ordinances were performed for his ancestors.

George Washington, the signers of the Declaration of Independence, and many other well-known men of the past appeared to him and asked him to do their temple ordinances for them. On August 21, 1877, Wilford Woodruff was baptized for all of the signers of the Declaration of Independence and fifty other prominent men, such as John Wesley and Columbus. He then baptized Brother John McAllister for every President of the United States except three. Of those, he said, ". . . and when their cause is just, somebody will do the work for them."

Two years later Wilford found it necessary to go into exile because the government was going to arrest those who were living plural marriage and put them in prison. He went to Arizona for two weeks and taught the Indians while he was there. Wherever he went, the Holy Ghost went with him, and he brought more of Heavenly Father's children into the Church.

During this period of time people who hated the Church decided they would destroy it once and for all. The long, hard trek across the plains did not bring them the peace they had come west for, and life was still hard for them. The government even had control of the land where the Salt Lake Temple now stands, and they had to pay rent to use their own property. Many of their leaders had to hide or be put in prison.

It was during this time of great persecution that Wilford Woodruff was called to be President of the Church. He was sustained in general conference on April 7, 1889, at the age of eighty-two.

Of this call he said, "This 7th day of April, 1889, is one of the most important days of my life, for I was made President of The Church of Jesus Christ of Latter-day Saints by unanimous vote of ten thousand of them. The vote was first taken by quorums and then by the entire congregation as in the case of President John Taylor. This is the highest office ever conferred upon any man in the flesh. It came to me in the eighty-third year of my life. I pray God to protect me and give me power to magnify my calling to the end of my days. The Lord has watched over me until the present time. I wish to counsel my wives and children and whoever may read this journal to honor God and keep His commandments to the end of their lives that they may receive eternal life and celestial glory in the presence of God and the Lamb."

During the nine years that he was President of the Church, he received the revelation discontinuing the practice of plural marriage, dedicated the Salt Lake Temple, established the Geneological Society, and changed the fast day from Thursday to the first Sunday of each month. In spite of the negative pressures around him, he worked steadfastly to build up the kingdom of God.

He also lived to see some important government changes that the Saints needed. In 1893, President Benjamin Harrison said they would no longer put the polygamists in prison if they had been married before November 1, 1890.

In 1891, Congress passed a resolution that gave Church property back to the Church, and Utah became a state.

President Woodruff was deeply loved by the people, and he loved them. His gospel sermons made them want to keep the commandments and live closer to their Father in Heaven.

He counseled the young people to "Live near to God; pray while young; learn to pray; learn to cultivate the Holy Spirit of God; link it to you and it will become a spirit of revelation to you, inasmuch as you nourish it."

Family life was a great source of happiness and contentment to President Woodruff. He loved to be home with his wives and children. His children laughed and played with their father, and they liked to have him read stories to them. If they did something wrong, he would discipline them, but he was not overly strict. They tried to follow his good examples of obedience, hard work, and faith.

THINK ABOUT IT:

1. What are some of the stories that show Wilford's great faith in our Heavenly Father?
2. What are some of the things that you admire most about Wilford Woodruff?
3. What are some of the characteristics that Wilford had that you plan to develop in your own life?

On the thirteenth of August, 1898, President Woodruff left Utah and went to San Francisco, California, to rest and regain his health and strength. He passed away there on September 2, 1898.

Though it has been many years since he passed away, his counsel for the young people can still influence their lives. He said, "I feel anxious to have our boys and girls, our young men and maidens, seek for that which is good. Whenever you are tempted to do evil, turn from it. Never make light of any of the commandments or ordinances of the gospel of Christ, and when you meet with any persons who do it, shun their society.

"Avoid the use of tobacco and strong drink, for they will lead to evil.

"You are laying the foundation while in the days of your youth, for a character which will decide your destiny through all time and throughout all eternity, either for good or evil."

Wilford Woodruff's entire life was an example of the principles he taught.

TESTIMONY

I bear my testimony that the Prophet Joseph Smith said before a large assembly in Illinois that if he was the emperor of the world and had control over the whole human family, he would sustain every man, woman, and child in the enjoyment of their religion. Those are my sentiments today. I bear my testimony that Joseph Smith was a true prophet of God, ordained of God to lay the foundation of His Church and Kingdom in the last dispensation and fulness of times. I bear by testimony that in the early spring of 1844, in Nauvoo, the Prophet Joseph Smith called the Twelve Apostles together and he delivered unto them the ordinances of the Church and the Kingdom of God; and all the keys and powers that God had bestowed upon him he sealed upon our heads. He told us that we must round up our shoulders and bear off this kingdom or we would be damned. I am the only man now living in the flesh who heard that testimony from his mouth, and I know this is true by the power of God manifest through him.

At that meeting, he began a speech of about three hours upon the subject of the Kingdom. His face was as clear as aspen, and he was covered with a power that I have never seen in an instant in the flesh before.

I bear testimony that Joseph Smith was the author of the endowments as received by the Latter-day Saints. I received my own endowments under his hands and direction and I know they are true principles. I not only received my own endowments under his hands, but I bear my testimony that Brigham Young, Heber C. Kimball, Willard Richards, George A. Smith, John Taylor, and other brethren received their endowments under the hands and direction of the Prophet Joseph—and also my wife Phoebe, Aunt Phoebe Smith, Leonora Taylor, Mary Smith, and others whose names I cannot recall now.

The Prophet Joseph laid down his life for the word of God and testimony of Jesus Christ, and he will be crowned as a martyr in the presence of God and the Lamb. In all his testimony to us the power of God was visibly manifest in the Prophet Joseph.

This is my testimony, spoken by myself into a talking machine on this the 19th day of March 1897, in the ninety-first year of my age.